Finicky Fish

by Kate Walker

illustrated by Bobbie Moynihan

Harcourt Achieve

Rigby • Saxon • Steck-Vaughn

www.HarcourtAchieve.com
1.800.531.5015

Characters

Jonah

Mom

Dad

Contents

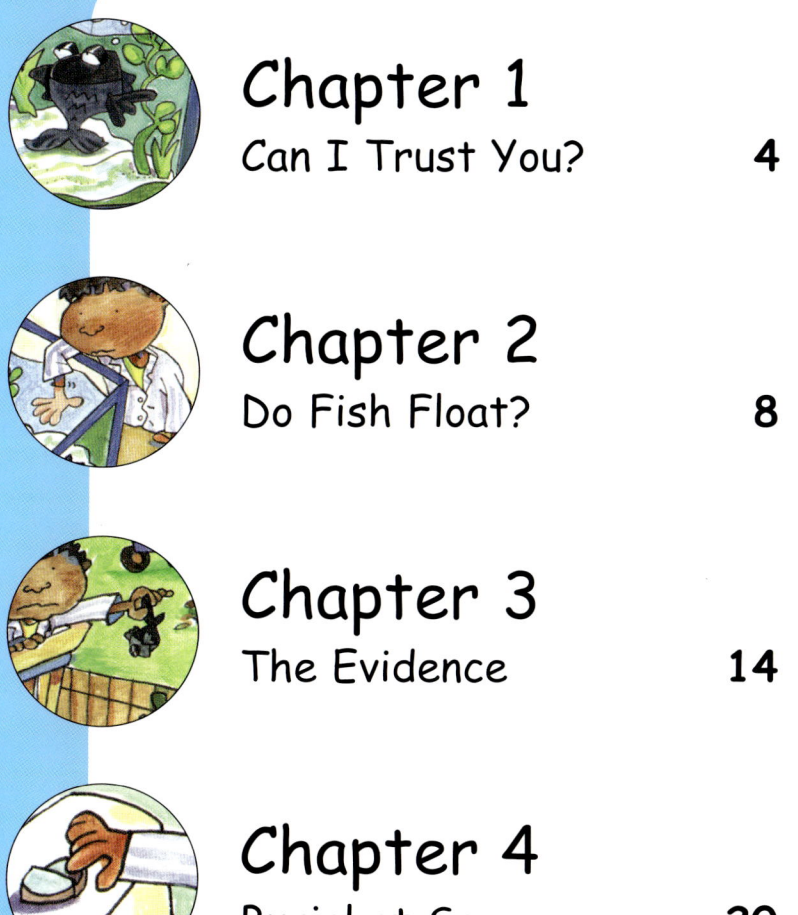

Chapter 1
Can I Trust You?   4

Chapter 2
Do Fish Float?   8

Chapter 3
The Evidence   14

Chapter 4
Burial at Sea   20

Chapter 1

Who Can You Trust?

Jonah's mother was given the present she'd always wanted — a tank full of beautiful fish. Fish with big bubble eyes!

They were very finicky fish.

They needed their light on for 12 hours a day. Their water temperature had to be just right. And they had to be fed at 6 p.m. on the dot, every day.

"Can I trust you to feed them for me?" Jonah's mother asked. His mom was a detective. She had to go away for a few days on a special case.

"No problem," said Jonah. "I'll set the alarm."

Then his favorite TV show came on. "I'll feed them during the ads," Jonah said.

Jonah forgot.

Do Fish Float?

The next morning, one of the finicky fish was floating on its back. It was the black one.

"Wake up!" Jonah said as he poked it.
Now the fish wasn't floating any more.
It fell to the bottom of the tank.

"Finicky fish!" said Jonah. He tossed in some fish food. "Come and get it!"

The other fish darted to the top. The black one stayed where it was. It sure looked dead. That meant he'd killed it!

Which was what his mother would do if . . .

. . . if she noticed.

There was only one thing to do. Get rid of the evidence and buy another fish.

Jonah reached into the tank. The fish lay in his hand like a lump of soggy cotton wool. He had hoped the fish was sleeping and would wake up.

He should make sure it was dead. Jonah put his ear against the fish's body. He could hear a glup-glup sound. Was that a fish's heartbeat?

Chapter 3

The Evidence

No, the fish was as dead as a dinosaur. Jonah carried it out to the balcony. He held it out over the rail, ready to drop it. But what if someone saw him?

He'd dig a hole in one of the potted plants instead.

But what would a detective think of when she saw freshly dug earth? A grave! His mom would spot it in an instant.

Jonah carried the soggy body into the kitchen. In came Kitty, looking for breakfast.

"Of course! Let the cat eat the evidence!" Jonah thought. This was turning into the perfect crime.

Jonah laid the fish in the cat's bowl. He waited around the corner. Kitty walked by, licking her lips. Jonah breathed a sigh of relief.

The cat picked up the fish and . . . spat it into her water bowl.

"Finicky cat!" Jonah grumbled.

Why couldn't his mom have normal pets? Jonah picked up the fish, just as he heard a yawn in the hall. His father was awake!

Burial at Sea

The shower in the bathroom came on. The sound of running water gave Jonah an idea. He darted up the hall and dropped the fish in the toilet. He closed the lid and pressed the flusher.

Burial at sea! What fish would mind that?
Then he nearly jumped out of his skin.

His father was banging on the wall.
"You know not to flush the toilet when someone's in the shower!" he shouted.

"Sorry!" Jonah yelled. "I forgot!"

The trouble was, now he needed to *use* the toilet. Well, he could go now, and flush it later. When Jonah lifted the lid . . .

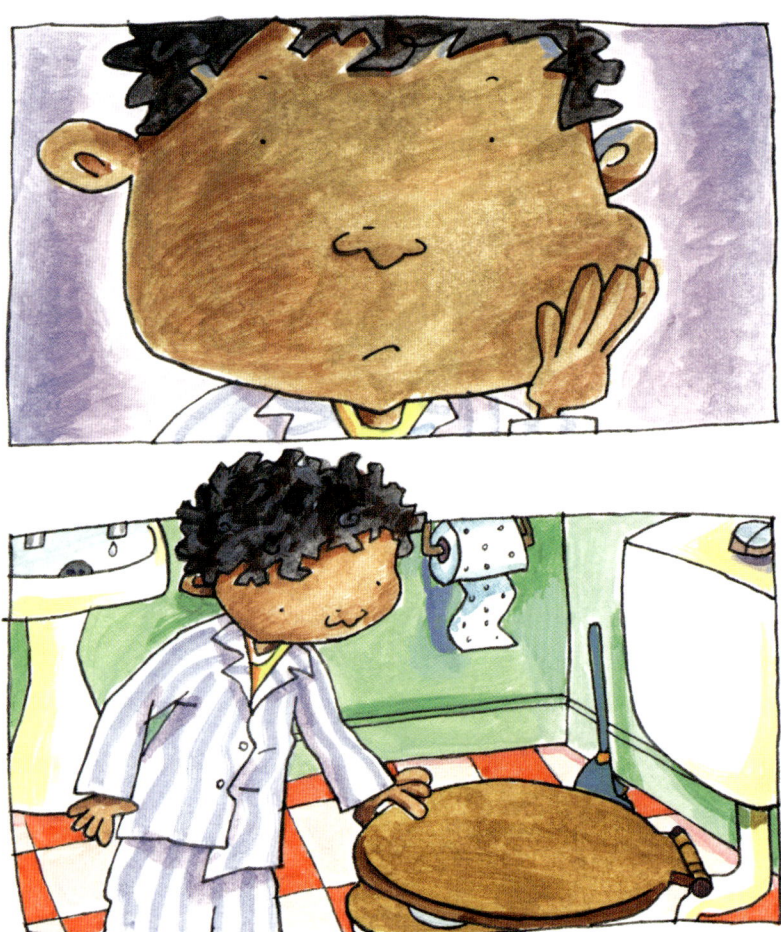

there was the little black fish, bobbing like a fishing boat.

The shower stopped. Jonah reached for the flusher again. And the fish in the bowl moved a fin! Then it moved its tail.

What if it were still alive? Jonah quickly reached into the toilet bowl. The fish felt like a lump of soggy toilet paper.

He held it close to his face and tried to see a heartbeat.

His father banged on the door. "Are you ready for school?"

Jonah jumped. The fish bounced off his head. It fell back into the toilet bowl.

"What are you doing in there?" his father called.

Jonah put his finger on the toilet flusher. The fish in the toilet bowl began to swim.

Jonah did the only thing he could. He burst out of the bathroom and confessed.

"I forgot to feed mom's fish. I thought one of them was dead, but now it's swimming in the toilet!"

"A fish in the toilet!" His father screwed up his face. "Well . . . you'll have to get it out and put it back in the tank!"

Jonah did. Then he set the alarm to ring, long and loud, at exactly 6 p.m.

"We'll have to tell Mom, won't we?"
Jonah asked.

"That one of her fish was in the toilet?" said Dad. "Let's not. You know how finicky she is."

Glossary

balcony
the outdoor area of an upper room or apartment

burial
putting something that has died into a grave

confessed
admitted to doing something wrong

crime
an action which breaks the law

detective
a person trained to discover who committed a crime

evidence
proof that something happened

finicky
fussy, choosy

grave
a hole in the ground where you bury the dead

instant
a very short time

temperature
how hot or how cold

Kate Walker

For her ninth birthday, my daughter, Josie, got a tank full of goldfish. The next morning, one was floating belly-up — dead! I knew she'd be upset, so I scooped it out and rushed to the toilet. Three times I flushed. That fish wouldn't go away. I didn't eat very much that day — not with a dead fish in my pocket.

Bobbie Moynihan